Learning Styles Response Form

For each pair of statements, circle the letter that represents the statement that comes closest to your current preference. Use a pencil or ballpoint pen and press firmly.

#										
1.	B	A								
2.	B	A								
3.	B	A								
4.	A	B								
5.	B	A								
6.	B	A								
7.	A	B								
8.	A	B								
9.			B	A						
10.			A		B					
11.			B	A						
12.			B	A						
13.				A	B					
14.			A		B					
15.				A	B					
16.				B	A					
17.			B		A					
18.				A	B					
19.			A		B					
20.			B	A						
21.						A	B			
22.						A		B		
23.						A		B		
24.						B	A			
25.							A	B		
26.						A		B		
27.							A	B		
28.							B	A		
29.						B	A			
30.							A	B		
31.						A		B		
32.						B	A			
33.									A	B
34.									A	B
35.									A	B
36.									B	A
37.									B	A
38.									B	A
39.									B	A
40.									A	B

D1361026

Learning Styles Scoring Form

Add the total number of "A"s and "B"s in each column and place that score in the total box at the bottom of the page. Then, transfer the total scores to page 5 of your Learning Styles Profile booklet.

	ATTENDING		TRANSLATING			RELATING			UNDERSTANDING	
1.	B	A								
2.	B	A								
3.	B	A								
4.	A	B								
5.	B	A								
6.	B	A								
7.	A	B								
8.	A	B								
9.			B	A						
10.			A		B					
11.			B	A						
12.			B	A						
13.				A	B					
14.			A		B					
15.				A	B					
16.				B	A					
17.			B		A					
18.				A	B					
19.			A		B					
20.			B	A						
21.						A	B			
22.						A		B		
23.						A		B		
24.						B	A			
25.							A	B		
26.						A		B		
27.							A	B		
28.							B	A		
29.						B	A			
30.							A	B		
31.						A		B		
32.						B	A			
33.									A	B
34.									A	B
35.									A	B
36.									B	A
37.									B	A
38.									B	A
39.									B	A
40.									A	B
Totals										
	Telescopic	Wide-angled	Dependent	Collaborative	Autonomous	Visual	Auditory	Kinesthetic	Global	Analytical

Learning Styles Profile

Dr. Jon Warner

HRD Press • Amherst • Massachusetts

Published by: HRD Press, Inc.
                 22 Amherst Road
                 Amherst, MA 01002
                 (800) 822-2801 (U.S. and Canada)
                 (413) 253-3488
                 (413) 253-3490 (Fax)
                 http://www.hrdpress.com

In association with Team Publications.

ISBN: 0-87425-799-9

Cover design by Eileen Klockars
Production services by Anctil Virtual Office

nstructions

.ll learners are not equal. They come in a variety of sizes, shapes, and cultures. Their past xperience and current ways of learning might also be very different. Some people like to process nformation through text, while others need visual support and images. Some learners best assimi- ate information alone. Others prefer to work in groups. There are people who can grasp information uickly and intuitively, and there are people who prefer to follow a strong sequential path and take me to reflect. In the end, the only thing you can say for sure is this:

Every individual learns in their own particular way.

his Learning Styles Profile will help every learner understand a little bit more about how they learn est and which teaching style is most effective for them.

he following pages contain 40 pairs of statements. For each pair, circle the letter corresponding to ne statement that most closely represents what is true for you most of the time (A or B). Mark your esponses on the Learning Styles Response Form, not in this booklet.

n some instances, both the "A" and the "B" statements will be appealing. Circle only one of them— ne statement that you believe comes **closest** to what is true for you. You might find that neither tatement is very characteristic; in such cases, circle the response that you feel to be **most** ccurate.

ry to respond as accurately as you can. This will help create a true profile and give you more ealistic information to analyze after you have plotted your scores and read the notes about ways make the most of every learning opportunity.

Learning Style Profile Statements

1. **B** I do not like to participate in workshops or training courses unless the subject really interests me.
   A I often find myself daydreaming when a trainer or facilitator is speaking.
2. **B** I can usually concentrate when I want to.
   A A noisy environment usually irritates me and breaks my concentration.
3. **B** I like to know what I will get out of it before I give my full attention.
   A I tend not to ask questions in a group of people, even if I do not understand.
4. **A** I ask questions to clarify information when it is needed.
   B I often find myself doodling or drawing.
5. **B** I find that diagrams and models are useful in training.
   A People often fidget a lot in the training room.
6. **B** I like to start and finish on time, and work hard in between.
   A I often think about things other than what is being discussed in a training class or workshop.
7. **A** People who talk and do not pay attention when they are in a class annoy me.
   B I sometimes need to be given instructions for activities or exercises twice.
8. **A** I try to look for the relevance of what is being presented.
   B Many course presenters are not very good at holding my attention.
9. **B** I often find other people's ideas more useful or interesting than my own.
   A In a formal training environment, I prefer to work with a group.
10. **A** I always like it when a trainer spells out clear learning objectives and outcomes.
    B In a formal training environment, I prefer to work independently.
11. **B** I prefer lectures to group activities or discussion.
    A I am happy to be given a wide range of pre-reading material before a course.
12. **B** In a formal training environment, I prefer to work with well-structured presentation notes and handouts.
    A You almost always meet really interesting people in a training class.
13. **A** I enjoy seminars in which ideas can be freely exchanged.
    B Some course leaders don't have all the information when you ask them questions.
14. **A** I am often attracted to a course that has a well-structured curriculum.
    B I could quite easily take courses on my own, via distance learning.
15. **A** I am happy to be given work assignments or projects involving one or two other people.
    B I like to set my own learning goals.
16. **B** I often volunteer for role-plays if they are part of a training course.
    A I usually decide pretty quickly which information is useful to me and which is not.
17. **B** I am happy to listen to a presentation that includes complex information.
    A I tend to study more effectively when I'm working with others.
18. **A** Learning is usually more effective when the subject is fully discussed or debated in a group.
    B I'm comfortable taking a leadership role in group discussions.
19. **A** I am rarely comfortable in loosely-defined brainstorming sessions.
    B I can often ask probing and incisive questions about the information that is being presented.

Learning Style Profile Statements

20. **B** I like to check facts or learning conclusions with others before I decide for myself.
    A I often get my best ideas by talking them out with others.
21. **A** When relaxing, I prefer to watch a film or go to see a play.
    B When relaxing, I prefer to listen to music or the radio.
22. **A** If I'm lost or need directions, I prefer having a map.
    B When relaxing, I prefer to play games or sports.
23. **A** I like course information presented in diagrams and pictures.
    B I often like to be doing something with my hands when I'm listening or talking.
24. **B** I prefer to talk to people face-to-face.
    A I am often impatient to speak, and I often finish other people's sentences.
25. **A** I enjoy talking to people on the phone for long periods of time.
    B I prefer many short breaks in a class so that I can move around.
26. **A** When bored, I tend to doodle or watch something.
    B I like to get involved in physical activity during a training class.
27. **A** If I'm lost or need directions, I need to be told.
    B I'm not good at sitting still for long periods of time.
28. **B** I am quite happy to listen to a long presentation or lecture.
    A If I am lost or in need of directions, I prefer to be shown the way.
29. **B** I tend to forget names and remember faces.
    A I find background music helpful when we are doing group exercises in a training class.
30. **A** I often forget faces but remember names.
    B I make gestures and use my hands when I am speaking.
31. **A** I'm not good at listening to others.
    B I like outdoor activities and exercises, where you can "get your hands dirty."
32. **B** I often find that a video is a useful addition to most courses.
    A I talk to myself sometimes.
33. **A** I am good at seeing the big picture.
    B It is important to include the details, as much as you can.
34. **A** I often see relationships between ideas.
    B It is usually best to focus and to concentrate.
35. **A** It is important to read between the lines.
    B I can often easily recall facts and figures.
36. **B** Learning presents lots of options and possibilities.
    A I like direct and practical answers to my questions.
37. **B** It is important to "go with the flow" most of the time.
    A I like things to be ordered in a step-by-step sequence.
38. **B** I don't like having to explain myself in detail.
    A I like to be prepared.
39. **B** I often don't know why I do some things.
    A I usually prefer to deal with one thing at a time.
40. **A** I quickly get bored when a course leader spends time on minor details.
    B I can get frustrated by opinion expressed as fact.

Graphing Your Profile Scores

Once you have read all 40 paired statements and circled your responses on the form, you will be ready to graph your learning styles profile. Separate the Response Form from the Scoring Form and follow the directions for scoring.

Your scores in four separate categories will create a profile of how you tend to learn, assimilate, and understand new information. The categories are:

1. How you **ATTEND** to new information or learning

2. How you **TRANSLATE** what you see, hear, and sense and make it meaningful

3. How you **RELATE** what is presented to what you already know

4. How you **UNDERSTAND** or synthesize the information and extrapolate it to use immediately or in the future.

These four categories represent four sequential steps in a natural cycle of learning and understanding whenever we are presented with information. Within these categories are a total of ten individual styles. We will use a graph on the next page to translate the scores from the Scoring Form.

Each of these ten styles (in their four respective categories) are represented by a horizontal line that runs from 0 *(no use is made of this style)* to 8 *(extremely high use is made of this style)*. Each of your total scores in the box at the bottom of the Scoring Form should be plotted on the graph. Once done, the bars can be shaded in up to these points to create your overall profile. This is best done with a colored felt-tip or highlighter pen.

As with many instruments of this kind, there are never any right or wrong answers in terms of individual scores, and there is no overall "optimal" profile. However, you can review your profile in relation to the gray bars already drawn on the graph, which represent average scores from previous users of this instrument. Your scores will be the same as the average in some areas, and lower or higher in others. Make a general comparative judgment about how your learning style differs from the way others learn.

Remember that we are all unique and complex in terms of how we choose to learn, absorb, and make use of new information. Do not think of high and low scores in each of the style bars as "good" or "bad." Think of your scores on the graph as a general indicator of your learning style in most circumstances, and try to think of ways to improve your skills in weak areas and change the learning process or environment to make the most of your preferred ways of learning.

Learning Style Categories

Name: _____ Date: _____

Attending (Motivation to Learn)

Telescopic	1 2 3 4 5 6 7
Wide-angled	1 2 3 4 5 6 7

Translating (Learning Reliance)

Dependent	1 2 3 4 5 6 7
Collaborative	1 2 3 4 5 6 7
Autonomous	1 2 3 4 5 6 7

Relating (Data Perception)

Visual	1 2 3 4 5 6 7
Auditory	1 2 3 4 5 6 7
Kinesthetic	1 2 3 4 5 6 7

Understanding (Information Synthesis)

Global	1 2 3 4 5 6 7
Analytical	1 2 3 4 5 6 7

The gray bars above reflect the average score or "norm" for all individuals who have taken this instrument at the time of printing.

Using the Learning Style Profile to Help You in the Future

This profile is designed to identify the learning style an individual uses in most situations. This instrument focuses on four areas:

1. **ATTENDING**
2. **TRANSLATING**
3. **RELATING**
4. **UNDERSTANDING**

In this profile, individuals will have scores in all four categories and sub-scales. Lets look at these four categories in more detail:

1. ATTENDING

The ATTENDING category looks at an individual's motivation to learn and the degree of commitment or concentration they tend to show when new information is presented to them. This category has two sub-scales: **Telescopic** and **Wide-angled. Telescopic** attending means that the individual is generally effective at concentrating and keeping his or her mind on the information, without worrying much about the physical context. **Wide-angled** attending means that the individual is often easily affected by environmental factors such as noise, low light, and other physical influences that can easily interfere with the flow of information.

2. TRANSLATING

The TRANSLATING category looks at who an individual relies on most to manage the transfer of learning and make coherent what they see, hear, or sense. This category has three sub-scales: **Dependent, Collaborative,** and **Autonomous. Dependent** means that the individual relies mainly on the trainer or facilitator for information. **Collaborative** means the individual relies mainly on group discussions and team activities for learning. **Autonomous** means that the individual mainly relies on himself or herself to manage the learning transfer process.

3. RELATING

The RELATING category looks at an individual's perception of data or information and how it is related to existing knowledge. There are three sub-scales in this category: **Visual, Auditory,** and **Kinesthetic. Visual** means that the individual prefers information that can be seen with the eyes. **Auditory** means that the individual prefers to have information that can be heard with the ears. **Kinesthetic** means that the individual prefers information that can be physically experienced, mainly through touch, smell, or taste.

4 UNDERSTANDING

The UNDERSTANDING category looks at an individual's preferences for synthesizing data or information that has been received. This category has two sub-scales: **Global** and **Analytical. Global** refers to a preference for understanding at a conceptual or big-picture level. **Analytical** refers to a preference for understanding at a detailed or step-by-step level.

Your Individual Score

Once you have answered the questions honestly and then accurately plotted your score, you should be in a position to:

1. Identify the ways you tend to learn.

2. Compare your style mix with the ways others learn, as shown on the graph.

3. Consider the implications for your future learning and think about how you can adjust your own approach to learning and influence the way that future learning is delivered to you.

As we said at the outset, there are no right or wrong answers when it comes to learning styles. In the final analysis, the essential value of any measurement instrument is the extent to which it provides a useful indicator of your personal way of operating. Identifying can help you make any adjustments or changes that you believe are necessary or desirable if you are to make the most of the learning experience.

Your scores will provide a useful basis for such a review. Whatever your results, carefully examine the results on all the scales. The next few pages contain general information about each category.

Interpreting Your Scores from the Learning Styles Profile

The following pages contain general indicators for each of the four categories and all ten of the sub-scales. They provide an overall guide as to how an individual learns or absorbs new information, based on their scores in each area.

ATTENDING

Attending characteristics refer to how an individual focuses or concentrates on new information or learning. Some individuals have a **telescopic** perspective: They can focus on the core message without noticing or being distracted by some of the ambient interference. However, they might miss some of the broader relevant signals. **Wide-angled** individuals tend to notice the complete learning environment, but side issues and distractions can interfere with the core message.

	Telescopic	Wide-angled
Physical climate	• Telescopic learners are likely to ignore most minor physical distractions without much difficulty. • They will try to adjust their learning climate themselves, wherever possible. • They are usually happy to work in any learning design formats and training-room design, as long as the course leader can be clearly seen and heard.	• Wide-angled learners are likely to find all but the most minor noises and interruptions irritating and distracting. • They expect the course leader to adjust the whole learning climate so that it is optimal. • They prefer a comfortable and appropriate learning format and layout, with lots of light and fresh air, and a room design that is conducive to learning.
Motivation	• Telescopic individuals are likely to set their own learning goals or objectives and tell others about them. • Motivation is self-generated and self-paced, and is quickly mustered. However, it can just as quickly disappear when the individual is not being challenged.	• Wide-angled individuals are likely to want pre-specified holistic learning objectives and goals explained early in the proceedings. • Motivation is driven by a coordinated effort to get the entire learning environment right—not just the content.
Level of concentration	• Concentration is high if there is a clear link with personal desires, but it will be low if too much time is wasted straying from the core messages of the learning. • Telescopic learners want learning goals and objectives and want someone to describe how to achieve them.	• Concentration is high if the complete training event is managed as a whole and care is taken to deal with all the learning issues, rather than just trying to "process" participants. • Wide-angled learners want learning to be nurtured in many ways and in the most appropriate learning environment.
	(55% of people)	**(45% of people)**

Interpreting Your Scores from the Learning Styles Profile

TRANSLATING

Translating characteristics focus on an individual's preferences for translating what they see, hear, or sense in a learning environment, and how they make the information intelligible in terms of their own existing mental models. **Dependent** learners expect the course leader to help them do this. **Collaborative** learners like to do this by talking about the issues raised in group sessions. **Autonomous** learners like to challenge assumptions and reflect on the information they gather on their own.

	The Dependent Learner	The Collaborative Learner	The Autonomous Learner
Overall characteristics	Dependent learners prefer leader-directed information, high structure, and clear focus. They prefer lectures or tutorials. Dependent learners tend to like large groups because the learning format has to be more formal.	Collaborative learners tend to favor discussion sessions, small-group seminars, and project work where there are assignments and opportunities for social interaction, games, simulations, case studies, and role plays.	The autonomous learner prefers to exercise an influence over the content and structure of the program. Autonomous learners think of the course leader/facilitator as a guiding resource. Guided reading and distance learning are comfortable formats.
General likes	• Tutorials • Lectures • Presentations • Bulletins • Manuals • Procedures • Work instructions • Guidelines • Outlines • Summaries	• Seminars • Workshops • Group discussions • Role plays • Think tanks • Brainstorming sessions • Projects • Games • Simulations • Clubs	• Reading • Writing • Distance learning • Simulations • One-to-one counseling • Models • Individual assignments • Loose ideas • Big-picture concepts
General dislikes	• Conceptual models • Doodles • Complex charts • Data without notes • Unsupported ideas/opinions	• Working alone • No interaction • Long lectures • Individual reading • Distance learning	• Technical presentations • Detailed lectures • Policies and procedures • Fixed procedures and work instructions • Workbooks/manuals

(52% of people)	(22% of people)	(26% of people)

Interpreting Your Scores from the Learning Styles Profile

RELATING

Relating characteristics focus on which "channels" individuals like to use the most when they relate new information to what they know (through short-term and long-term memory). The three primary channels are **Visual, Kinesthetic,** and **Auditory.** Most individuals use all three channels, but given a preference, we all tend to favor one.

VISUAL LEARNERS (45% OF PEOPLE)

- When relaxing, prefer to watch a movie, DVD, or video, go to a play, or read a book.
- Prefer to talk to people face-to-face.
- Are often fast thinkers and talkers.
- Forget names, but remember faces.
- If lost or need directions, prefer a map.
- When inactive, tend to doodle or watch someone/something.
- Praise with a note, letter, or card.

Learn best by:

- Writing down key facts.
- Visualizing what they are learning.
- Creating pictures/diagrams from what they are learning.
- Using timelines to remember dates.
- Creating their own strong visual links.
- Using pictures, diagrams, charts, film, video, graphics, etc.

KINESTHETIC LEARNERS (25% OF PEOPLE)

- When relaxing, prefer to play games and sports.
- Prefer to talk to people while they do something else.
- Are slow talkers, and use gestures and expressions.
- Shake hands with people they meet.
- If lost or in need of directions, prefer to be shown the way.
- Praise people with a physical pat on the back.
- Cannot sit still for long periods of time.

Learn best by:

- Copying demonstrations and performing role plays.
- Making models.
- Recording information as they hear it, perhaps on a mind map.
- Walking around while they read.
- Underlining/highlighting new information/ key points.
- Putting key points on index cards and organizing them.
- Getting physically and actively involved in their learning.

AUDITORY LEARNERS (30% OF PEOPLE)

- When relaxing, prefer to listen to music or the radio.
- Prefer to talk to people on the phone.
- Enjoy listening to others, but are impatient to talk; tend to speak in a rhythmic voice.
- Forget faces, but remember names.
- If lost or in need of directions, prefer to be told.
- When inactive, tend to talk to themselves or others.
- Praise people verbally.

Learn best by:

- Hearing a seminar, presentation, or explanation.
- Reading aloud to themselves.
- Reading with emotion, inflection, or accent.
- Making a tape of key points to listen to in the car, while ironing, etc.
- Verbally summarize in their own words.
- Explain the subject to someone else.
- Use their own internal voice to verbalize what they are learning.

Interpreting Your Scores from the Learning Styles Profile

UNDERSTANDING

Understanding characteristics have to do with how individuals like to ultimately synthesize the information they receive and extrapolate it for their own theoretical or practical use. The two ways most people do this are globally and analytically. **Global** synthesizers take a big-picture and conceptual view and broadly absorb information. **Analytical** synthesizers, on the other hand, are likely to make sense of learning by breaking it down logically and step-by-step.

GLOBAL SYNTHESIZERS	ANALYTICAL SYNTHESIZERS
Strengths: • See the big picture • See relationships • Cooperate in group efforts • Read between the lines • See many options • Paraphrase • Do several things at once • Read body language • Get others involved	**Strengths:** • Are detailed • Are focused • Are organized • Remember specifics • Provide direct answers • Are consistent • Are objective • Are individually competitive • Do one thing at a time
Style: • Are often more sensitive to other people's feelings • Are flexible • Go with the flow • Learn by discussion and by working with others • Need reassurance and reinforcement • Are future-focused and expansive in thinking • Try to avoid conflict • Might skip steps and details	**Style:** • Like things ordered step-by-step • Pay close attention to details • Must be prepared • Need to know what to expect • Often value facts over feelings • Prefer to finish one thing at a time • Rarely become personally or emotionally involved • Are logical • Find the facts, but sometimes miss the main idea
Frustrations: • Having to explain themselves analytically • Not getting a chance to explain themselves • Not knowing the reason for doing something • Having to do something step-by-step without first knowing where they'll end up • Not being able to relate what they are learning to their own situation • Having to show the steps they used to get an answer	**Frustrations:** • When opinion is expressed as fact • Do not always understand the purpose for doing something • Having to listen to an overview without first knowing the steps involved • Having to listen to an explanation, when all that's needed is a "yes" or a "no" answer • Having to deal with generalities • Having to find the meaning in what they learn • Not being able to finish one task before going on to the next
(53% of people)	**(47% of people)**

Summary

Actually evaluating what we hear, see, or experience is a complex process. We bring to each new situation our own history, preferences, biases, and skills. Our mental learning evaluation cycle is a four-step process:

STEP 1   (A pre-condition of learning) We first filter out inhibitors and attend to the subject with our full attention. This is predominantly a right-brained activity: We appraise the broad context within which the information should be evaluated (ATTENDING).

STEP 2   Then we translate the information in a way that matches our existing knowledge or mental models of the way things work. In some cases, we will have to unlearn something before we can encode or encrypt the new learning to be meaningful. This is predominantly a left-brain activity, connected with logic and reason (TRANSLATING).

STEP 3   Now we must relate the information to existing patterns or blocks of knowledge in our short-term or long-term memory in order to connect new information with the old information in the same place. This is predominantly a right-brain activity, connected with associated general ideas and relationships (RELATING).

STEP 4   Finally, we must summarize the new information in connection with the old, and distill it for future access and use when we need it. This is predominantly a left-brain activity, connected with induction and deduction processes (UNDERSTANDING).

Our minds can go through the entire learning evaluation cycle in a few seconds, but if the information is complex or confusing, it will take longer. If we travel the cycle successfully, our "self-talk" or internal reflection will be positive and we will be able to add to our knowledge and take action (if we so choose). However, if we stall at any of these steps or travel this cycle with difficulty, our self-talk is likely to be negative or at least confused. We can then introspectively travel the cycle again to see if we can work out the problem.

The purpose of this profile is to provide you with some useful guidance on how you personally travel through these four steps in your own learning cycle. This four-step model is illustrated on the next page.

EFFECTIVE LEARNING: CYCLE

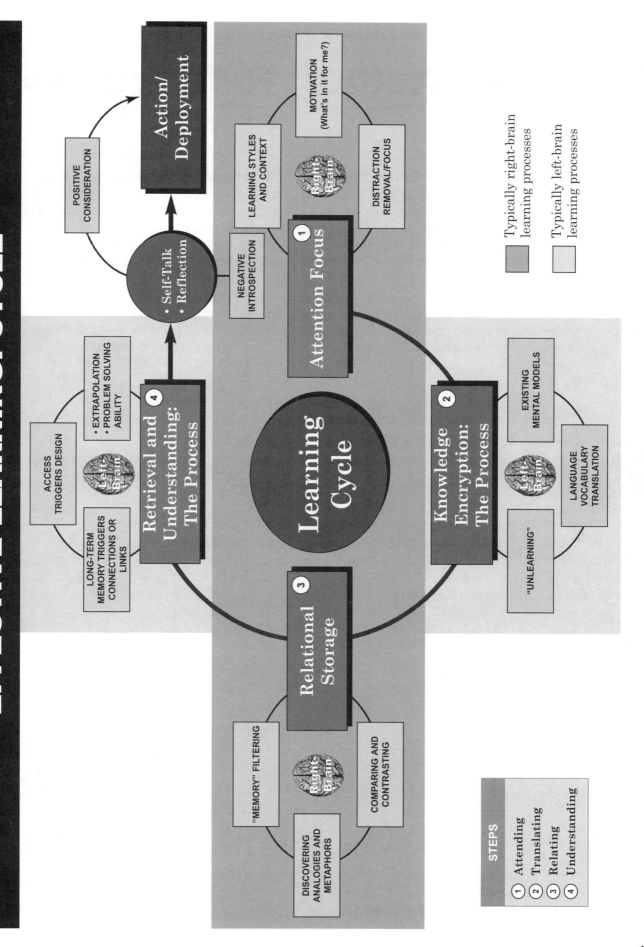

Action/Deployment

POSITIVE CONSIDERATION

- Self-Talk
- Reflection

NEGATIVE INTROSPECTION

Learning Cycle

1 Attention Focus

MOTIVATION (What's in it for me?)

LEARNING STYLES AND CONTEXT

Right Brain

DISTRACTION REMOVAL/FOCUS

2 Knowledge Encryption: The Process

EXISTING MENTAL MODELS

Left Brain

LANGUAGE VOCABULARY TRANSLATION

"UNLEARNING"

3 Relational Storage

"MEMORY" FILTERING

Right Brain

COMPARING AND CONTRASTING

DISCOVERING ANALOGIES AND METAPHORS

4 Retrieval and Understanding: The Process

ACCESS TRIGGERS DESIGN

Left Brain

- EXTRAPOLATION
- PROBLEM SOLVING ABILITY

LONG-TERM MEMORY TRIGGERS CONNECTIONS OR LINKS

Typically right-brain learning processes

Typically left-brain learning processes

STEPS
1 Attending
2 Translating
3 Relating
4 Understanding

13

About the Author; References

ABOUT THE AUTHOR

Jon Warner is a professional manager with over 20 years' experience working with multinational companies in the United Kingdom, Europe, the United States, and Australia. He has been the senior staff member in human resources departments, and has held several professional leadership positions with responsibility for large groups of employees. Jon has in recent years been involved in wide-ranging organizational consultancy work and the pursuit of best-practices leadership for such major organizations as Mobil Oil, Quantas, United Energy, Dow Corning, Coca Cola, Barclays Bank, National Bank, Honda, BTR, Gas and Fuel, Air Products and Chemicals, and Caltex.

Jon is managing director of Team Publications PTY Limited, an international training and publishing company committed to bringing practical and fun-to-use learning material to the worldwide training market, such as the One Page Coach® integrated training packages. He holds a master's degree in Business Administration and a Ph.D. in organizational change and learning, and lives and works on Australia's Gold Coast.

REFERENCES FOR LEARNING STYLES

Knowles, M. (1990). *The adult learner: a neglected species.* Gulf.

Gregoric, A. (1985). *Inside styles.* Gabriel Systems.

Dunn, R. (1984). *Learning styles: The start of science.* Theory Into Practice.

Blakeslee, T. (1980). *The right brain.* Doubleday.

Tobias, C. (1994). *The way they learn.* Word Books.

Burns, R. (1995). *The adult learner at work.* Business and Professional Publishing.

Honey, P., Mumford A. (1992). *The manual of learning styles.* Maidenhead.

Silver, H., Strong, R., Pereni, M. (1997). *Integrating learning styles and multiple intelligences.*

Sadler-Smith, E. (1996). *Learning styles: a holistic approach.* Journal of Industrial Training.

Kolb, D. (1984). *Experiencial learning.* Prentice-Hall.